FASTS OF THE HINDUS AROUND THE WEEK

(Background stories, ways of performance & their importance)

J.N. Kaushik

BOOKS FOR ALL
Delhi-110052

Sales Office:
D.K. PUBLISHERS DISTRIBUTORS (P) LTD.
1, Ansari Road, Darya Ganj, New Delhi-110002
Phones: 3261465, 3278368
Fax: (011) 3264368

First Edition 1992
Second Edition 1995

ISBN 81-7386-129-3

Published by: **BOOKS FOR ALL**
[A Division of D.K. Publishers Distributors (P) Ltd.]
at Regd.Off.: A-6, NIMRI Community Centre,
Ashok Vihar, Phase-IV, Delhi-110052.

Typeset by:
ABC for DTP, Delhi-34

Printed at
D K Fine Art Press P Ltd.
Delhi-110052

Printed in India

Preface

Preserving national culture should be a matter of pride because the edifice of the present society stands on the foundation laid by our ancestors. The importance of our cultural heritage has rightly been emphasized in our National Policy of Education (1986).

The Indian culture has been preserved and handed over to progenies through oral preachings. The main aim and objective of this practice was to inculcate in people eternal values like chastity, truthfulness, donation to the needy, helping and serving the elders, good family relations, respect for women, kindness towards all creatures - big or small, preserving nature and natural objects, accepting the nature's gifts as boons, fair dealing with all, devotion or bhakti, shedding hatred, pride, jealousy, anger etc. This was attained through observing fasts and leading a disciplined life and controlling diet and food habits.

The present collection of cultural and religious stories is an attempt to bring to light our oral culture. There is every possibility that some critics may find in these stories certain dogmas, misbeliefs or unscientific attitude towards life. But this is a literature which was meant for an average folk who had no time for higher thoughts or pursuits of life. These stories need fresh interpretations.

The Week Days' stories have special significance in as much as they propose a weekly engagement for the common folk and specially for the women folk. Each day of the week brings a special message. These stories have given solace to millions of people from time immemorial.

Before concluding, it would be worthwhile to explain as to how a particular day of the week was allotted to particular star or planet. According to Indian astronomers, the position of the planets, in order of their placement in the sky, is - Shani, Vrihaspati, Mangal, Ravi, Shukra, Budha and Chandrama. They rotate in their own orbits or paths.

The sun was visible on the first dawn upon this earth. This 'hora' or hour was dedicated to this planet. People called it Ravivar or Adityavar i.e. Sun's day. In the second 'hora' or hour, the other planets appeared in quick succession in the rotation as referred to above. In the 24th 'hora' or hour, moon appeared in the sky. So this day was named as Somvar, Chandravar or Moon's day. Likewise other planets followed this pattern and the days were named after them which appeared in the first hour of the succeeding dawn. So 'Shani' was the deity of the dawn on the 7th day.

These stories are mainly related in the Central part of India and especially in the Hindi and Punjabi speaking belts.

J.N. Kaushik

Contents

1

Ravivar Ki Kahani-I

(Surya Narain)

(People keep fast on Sundays in the name of Surya Narain or the Sun God. They take food only once a day, generally fruit, before sun-set. Saltish and fried items are avoided. It is believed that a fast on a Sunday saves one from skin diseases like leprosy, ringworm, and eye sores. Sun God is worshipped with red sandalwood and red flowers. This story is related with Surya Narain.)

Once the Sun God or Surya Narain ruled this world. He looked after both the world and his family. He fed one and all from the same spoon. He gave half a spoon to all the creatures on the earth and the other half to his family.

The members of Surya Narain's family did not work hard and washed away his blessings. Once Surya Narain's wife said to her mother-in-law, "Your son does not give enough food to us. You go and tell him that he should give us more food."

Surya Narain's mother went to her son and said, "Your wife says that the food given by you is not enough for us. Increase the supply."

Surya Narain smiled and said, "Dear mother, I give half a spoon of food to all the creatures and the remaining half to your family. I have no more food to give."

The mother came back and said, "He is helpless in increasing the supply. Better you go yourself and convince him."

Surya Narain's wife made for her husband's court. The courtiers welcomed her. Surya Narain made her sit by his side and listened to her difficulties.

Surya Narain's wife insisted on larger supply for her family. Surya Narain smiled and said, "Your family members do not work hard. They do not even clean the house properly. Take these five dices and play with your neighbours. You will find surplus food for your family."

Surya Narain's wife returned home with the dices. She was happy that she would show the dices to her neighbours and play with them.

It was Sunday morning. She took the dices to her neighbours, but found to her great surprise that they were busy at work right from the sunrise. Some of them were cleaning or dusting their houses. Others were milking their cows or doing petty household work. None talked with her.

She took courage and entered one of the houses and requested the people there to play with her. The lady of the house said, "I am on Sunday fast. I am to clean my house and prepare food for worship."

Surya Narain's wife said, "How does this fast help you?"

The lady said, "Because of it, I have developed a habit for early rising, keeping the house clean, behaving well with every body and remembering God."

Surya Narain's wife said, "What is the way for keeping this fast?"

The lady told her that it was simple. She advised her to take rice before the sun-set and avoid salty and fried dishes.

Surya Narain's wife decided to keep fast on all Sundays. In a short period, she became prosperous.

Once Surya Narain decided to test his wife's integrity. He disguised himself as an old Pandit and visited his house. He asked for some food. His wife said, "I am on fast. You will have to wait till evening." The Pandit agreed.

By evening, the food was ready. The Pandit said, "I shall take my meals in the same dish in which Surya Narain used to take."

Surya Narain's mother became angry. But his wife agreed to serve him in the same dish. It was night. The old man said, "I shall sleep on the same bed which Surya Narain uses. Surya Narain's wife will press my feet also."

Although Surya Narain's mother became angry, his wife agreed to press his feet. As the night advanced, the old man asked her to share bed with him. She sensed the reality and shared the bed with him.

From now onwards, the Pandit visited her house every Sunday. The lady became pregnant. Everybody talked ill of her. She gave birth to a child. It was too much for her mother-in-law.

Her mother-in-law said, "This is lechery. This is impious and immoral. Your husband will not forgive you."

The lady said, "The old man who visits me at night is no one else but Surya Narain himself."

The mother-in-law said, "You will have to undergo a test. Are you ready for it?"

The lady agreed.

The mother-in-law brought an unspinned, *kachcha*, thread. She tied its one end to a tree and hung the other end in a deep dingy well. She asked Surya Narain's wife to go to the brink of the well. Surya Narain' wife caught hold of the thread and put her legs inside the well. It was too much for the onlookers.

All of a sudden, Surya Narain appeared on the scene. He caught hold of her hand and narrated the whole story to his mother. The onlookers were pleased.

Surya Narain now led a happy and prosperous life with his family members.

RAVIVAR KI KAHANI – II

(Sun and the Divine Cow)

(This story of the Sun God, is related on the occasion of Sunday fast. It depicts the importance of cow and cow dung and suggests the victory of innocence over jealousy.)

Once there was an old lady. She would get up early in the morning and took her bath. She kept her house clean by plastering it with cow dung, and took her meals only after offering food to the Sun God. She lived a happy life.

This lady used to collect cow dung from her neighbour's house. The neighbour's wife was jealous of her. She tethered her cow inside the room so that the old lady could not collect the dung.

And as she could not plaster her house with cow-dung, she did not cook her food. She did not even offer food to the idols. She remained on fast throughout the day and slept with empty stomach.

The Sun God appeared before her in her dream. He said, "Why did not you take your meals? Why did you not offer food to the idols?"

The old lady said politely, "My neighbour's lady did not allow me to collect cow-dung from her house. I could not clean my house. I have no cow of my own."

The Sun God said, "I am happy with you because you kept fast on Sunday. I am pleased with your worship. I shall give you a beautiful cow."

The god disappeared. The old lady opened her eyes. A beautiful milch cow with a calf was there in her courtyard. She was surprised to see them. She arranged hay and water for them.

When the neighbour's lady saw the cow in the old lady's house, she became jealous of her. She also noticed that the cow's dung was of gold and not an ordinary dung. She took the gold dung and replaced it with the ordinary dung of her cow. She continued the replacing practice for a number of days.

The Sun God noted that the old lady was being cheated by her neighbour. He caused a storm at sun-set. The old lady tethered her cow inside her room for its safety. She was, however, surprised to see that her cow gave her gold dung instead of an ordinary one. She could see through her neighbour's trick.

The neighbour's lady was constantly jealous. She thought of a plan to deprive her of the wonder cow. She went to the king and said, "My Lord, a poor old lady in our neighbourhood has a divine cow. The cow gives gold dung. It would be befitting for your graciousness if this cow is with you. She keeps it inside her room. No one can have even its glimpse."

The king was a greedy person. He told his courtier, "Go immediately and bring the cow."

The old lady was about to offer food to the Sun God's idol when the courtier reached her house. He untied the rope from peg and took away the cow. The lady prayed and wept, but all in vain.

The old lady missed her meals that day. She prayed to her God for the safe return of the cow. She could not sleep at night.

The king on the other hand, was highly pleased to have that divine cow. That night, he had a dream. The Sun God was there who said, "I offered this cow to the old lady as a token of my affection for her worship of me. You do not deserve this cow."

The king woke up. He was badly shaken. He saw that the entire palace was full of cow dung. There was bad smell all around.

In the morning, the king sent for the old lady with due honour. He returned the cow to the old lady and also gave her some wealth. The neighbour's lady was suitably punished which was a cause of relief to all.

The king proclaimed order that all his subjects should observe fast on Sundays if they wanted their desires to be fulfilled. Now, all his people were prosperous. Illness never visited them. They never faced any natural calamity. Everyone enjoyed happiness.

2

Somvar Ki Kahani-I

(Lord Shiva - The Diety of Monday)

(This story is connected with Monday fast. Monday fast is practised to propitiate Lord Shiva. It has special significance in the month of Shravan. Meals are taken only once a day, generally after midday. It is believed that Monday fast results in happy family life and acquisition of knowledge.)

Once upon a time, there was a poor Brahman. He had nothing to sustain his family.

One day his wife said to him, "My Lord, can't you go out for earning money? We are in need of food."

The Brahman said, "It is my pious duty to feed you all. I have no income. I shall go out to make some income. Give me my *lota* (brass pot) and string."

The Brahman's wife gave him his *lota* and string and he started on his journey. There was a big peepal tree. It was beside a cross-road on the *Kachcha* path. He raised a small platform around the tree and meditated there for twelve long years. The passers-by offered him food.

Lord Shiva was pleased with his prayers and Monday fasts. He disguised himself as a *Swami,* an ascetic, with a *dandi* (staff) in his hand. He came near the peepal tree where the Brahman was meditating.

The Brahman opened his eyes. A Dandi Swami stood before him, blessing him with his raised hands.

The Swami said, "What is your desire? You can ask for some boon."

The Brahman was overwhelmed and said, "I have nothing to support my family. I need money."

The Dandi Swami said, "Worldly possessions are temporary. I shall give you a valuable *Mantra.* It will help you fulfil all your desires."

The Brahman said, "What is that *Mantra,* O Swamiji?"

The Swami said, "The Mantra is Tuesday, Wednesday, Thursday, Friday, Saturday and Sunday, all are related with one or the other deity. Lord Shiva is the deity of Monday. Whosoever knows this secret gets nine treasures of *Kubera,* the Lord of Wealth, as also all the *Riddhis* and *Siddhis* i.e. prosperity, wealth etc."

Having got the Mantra, the old Brahman was happy. His sister's village was nearby. He thought of going to her. The sister was surprised to see her brother. She said, "You have given me a pleasant surprise. What brings you here? You have visited my house after a long time." The Brahman said, "Let us sit down and talk about our family matters."

The sister replied, "I have no spare time to sit and talk. There are a lot of things to be done. I shall borrow a handful flour from my neighbour and cook food for you."

The brother said, "Clean and plaster your house with the cow dung first and light the holy lamp. Invite your neighbours. Put on new clothes, I shall tell you a valuable Mantra."

The old lady went from door to door to invite her neighbours. Many women gathered there to listen to the valuable Mantra.

The old Brahman said, "Tuesday, Wednesday, Thursday, Friday, Saturday and Sunday are related with one or other deities. Lord Shiva is the deity of Monday. Whosoever knows this secret gets nine treasures of Lord *Kubera*, the lord of wealth, as also all Riddhis and Siddhis."

To the great surprise of all gathered there, as soon as the Mantra was used, the Brahman's sister house got filled with a variety of household articles and enormous wealth. It was a pleasant surprise for the Brahman also, because he had tested the Mantra for the first time.

The Brahman's sister was now happy. She said, "Take your meals and have some rest."

The Brahman said, "I will not take my meals in your house because you are younger than me. I shall take my meals at my family priest's house."

On his way back home, he met his Baniya friend. He repeated the same Mantra there also. The Baniya's house also got filled with wealth.

The Brahman returned to his village. His wife was surprised to see him empty-handed. "You are here after twelve long years and still you have nothing with you", she said. "What is the matter?"

The Brahman said, "I have learnt a valuable Mantra from a Dandi Swami. The Mantra is more valuable than wealth.

The Brahman's wife got infuriated but the Brahman made her listen to the Mantra. As the Brahman recited the Mantra, by the grace of Lord Shiva, his house got filled with wealth.

The Brahman's wife was surprised to see such an immense wealth. "What shall we do with all this wealth?" She remarked.

The Brahman replied. "This wealth should be spent for the good of others. Let wells be dug all along the road-side to facilitate the travellers quench their thirst. Let marriages of all the poor unmarried girls be arranged by us."

Somvar Ki Kahani - II

(This story is connected with Monday fast. Those who observe Monday fast listen to this story in the afternoon after offering prayers to Lord Shiva.)

Once there lived a wealthy merchant in a city. He always had immense wealth and prosperity. But despite all the worldly possessions, he remained sad because he had no son. He regularly observed Monday fast to have a son. He used to go to the Shiva temple and worshipped there Lord Shiva and Goddess Parvati with full faith. Goddess Parvati was pleased at his devotion.

She implored Lord Shiva and said, "My Lord, this wealthy merchant is your faithful devotee. He regularly observes Monday fast but still he has no son. Please fulfil his desire."

Hearing the implorings of Parvati, Lord Shiva said, "Let your desire be fulfilled. I grant him a boon. He will be the father of a son, but ....."

"Why but my Lord?" asked Parvati.

Lord Shiva said, "but he will live for twelve years only."

Fortunately, this wealthy merchant could hear their conversation. As time passed on, the merchant's wife gave birth to a beautiful son. He celebrated his son's birth with great pomp and show and distributed food, clothes and money among the poor. All prayed for his son's long and happy life. But the merchant was still sad because he knew that his son would not live beyond twelve years. Yama, the god of Death, spares none. Knowing what the situation was, the merchant started observing the Monday fast with greater zest and there was no let up in the worship of Lord Shiva. He practised all the rites of worship.

At the age of eleven, the merchant's son looked quite smart and mature. All desired that he should be married to a beautiful girl. The merchant's wife also wanted her son's marriage. She insisted for it again and again.

The merchant did not agree to this proposal. He sent for his brother-in-law and said, "Accompany my son to Kashiji. Arrange for his best spiritual knowledge. Take enough money from my treasure. Arrange devotional gatherings on your way to Kashiji at every halt and distribute alms among the beggars."

The merchant's son started his journey for Kashi with his maternal uncle. They arranged devotional gatherings and distributed clothes at every halting camp. They also arranged best eats for the Brahmans and made enough offerings to them.

One day they made a halt at a capital of a king. The king's daughter's marriage was to take place that day. The marriage party had already reached the city. The bridegroom's party was terribly disturbed because the bridegroom was blind of one eye. They were in search of a beautiful boy to replace him.

The bridegroom's father sent his men in search of a beautiful boy. The men spotted the merchant's son who was camping in an inn with his maternal uncle. The bridegroom's father was a rich person. He said to the merchant's maternal uncle, "My prestige is at stake. I need a handsome bridegroom in place of my one-eyed son. I shall give enough wealth if your ward agrees to have a temporary marriage with the king's daughter. He shall be free immediately after the marriage ceremony is over."

The merchant's brother-in-law convinced his sister's son for a temporary marriage. The bride's party praised their luck when they saw a handsome bridegroom with the marching band at the head of the marriage procession.

The merchant's son and the king's daughter were married around the holy fire. At the time of departure, the merchant's son picked his bride's scarf and wrote, "Now we are husband and wife. I am not the son of a king. I am the son of a rich merchant. I was on way to Kashiji for spiritual studies. Your real bridegroom is blind of one eye."

The bride noticed her bridegroom writing something on the scarf. She could not read his message at that time. When the marriage party was about to depart, the bride read the message. She was shocked to know the reality. She refused to accompany with the one-eyed bridegroom. The marriage party returned without a bride.

The merchant's son reached Kashiji and devoted himself fully to the spiritual studies. His maternal uncle arranged devotional gatherings and gave donations everyday for the well-being of his sister's son.

On the last day of the twelfth year, the merchant's son felt pain in the chest. His maternal uncle was performing the religious rites as per his routine. As he went inside the room, he found the boy dead. He was full of grief, but kept silent as the Brahmans would not accept food from such a house. With courage, he completed his routine.

When his routine was over, he started crying. Many people gathered around him and shared his grief.

Fortunately, Lord Shiva and Parvati were also passing by that house. When Parvati heard the cries and beating of breast, her motherly compassion got aroused. She was a mother, after all. Having known the facts, she said to Lord Shiva, "My dear Sire, please ask Yama to return his life. Yama is always at your command. Please do this favour to me. You are the protector of all creatures."

Lord Shiva agreed and sprinkled Ganga water on the dead body. The boy got up as if he was making an excuse for sleep.

The spiritual education of the merchant's son was over. They started their journey homeward. They arranged spiritual discourses and distributed alms among the needy throughout their way. Now, they were back in the city where this boy was married. The king recognised the boy immediately. He took him to his palace with full honour and on an auspicious day, he arranged to happy departure for his daughter. He also gave adequate dowry.

The merchant's son reached his city alongwith his bride. His father could not believe it. He was sitting on the roof of a big mansion with his wife, waiting for his son. They had decided that they would not come down until their son supported them himself; otherwise they would commit suicide by jumping down the roof.

So the merchant's son alongwith his bride went up to the roof. They touched their feet. The merchant and his wife were very happy to see the couple.

Somvar Ki Kahani - III

(Monday Fasts for Sixteen Weeks)

(This story is related at the time of breaking Monday fast. Unshakeable belief in Lord Shiva brings prosperity and nonbelievers get sufferings. If the husband and wife have the same belief, they are bound to lead a happy life. Even repentance at some stage is as good).

Once Lord Shiva visited the famous city of Amravati. Parvati also accompanied him. On their way, they saw a beautiful Shiva temple and decided to spend some time there.

One day, Parvati found Lord Shiva in a playful mood. She said to him, "O my Lord, let us have a dice game." Lord Shiva obliged her and the game started.

Meanwhile, the priest of the temple had come there. Parvati turned towards him and said "Please foretell who will win this game?"

The Brahman gave no serious thought to her question and abruptly said, "Lord Shiva will win the game."

Incidentally Parvati won the game. She was angry because the Brahman had told a lie. Lord Shiva tried to pacify her, but she cursed the Brahman that he be a leper.

In due course, the Brahman became a leper and spent a miserable life. After some time a few fairies descended on the earth and pitied the fate of the priest. On asking him, the priest narrated the whole episode. One of the fairies said, "You observe Monday fasts for sixteen weeks without break. On the seventeenth Monday, prepare some holy food or 'Prasaad' with flour mixed with '*ghee*' and '*gur*'. Distribute this *prasaad* among the members of your family and take some yourself. You will be free from this 'leprosy'.

The fairies disappeared and the priest followed the instructions. Soon, he regained his normal health.

Once Lord Shiva and Parvati again visited that temple. Parvati was surprised to see the priest. He was his normal self. She enquired about this feat and the priest narrated the whole story.

Parvati was happy, she also decided to observe Monday fasts for sixteen weeks. Incidentally, on the seventeenth Monday, when she broke her fast, her beloved son Kartikeya, who was displeased with her, appeared and said, "O dear mother what is that power with which you have called me? What is the mystery?"

Parvati said, "O my dear son, all this miracle is due to observing Monday fasts for sixteen weeks without interruption."

Kartikeyas' Brahman friend had been in a foreign land for quite some time. Kartikeya said, "I shall observe Monday fasts for sixteen weeks for happy reunion with my friend."

He observed the 16 weeks fasts as per rules and to his great surprise his friend returned hale and hearty.

The friend enquired about the miracle and Kartikeya told him the modalities to be observed for Monday fast. The Brahman friend was very curious about his marriage. He decided to observe the Monday fasts for sixteen weeks.

On the seventeenth Monday, the Brahman friend went to a city. The ruler of the city decided to marry his daughter to a person on whose neck his well-decorated elephant would put the garland. The Brahman joined the show. Incidentally, the elephant garlanded him. The ruler of the city gave him his daughter and also a lot of money.

The couple departed the next day and were back in their home. On the honeymoon night, the bride said, "O my dear, how is it that the elephant ignored all the princes and garlanded you? How did you succeed on the auspicious moments?"

The bridegroom said, "I observed fasts on sixteen Mondays. Monday is Lord Shiva's day. It is due to his blessings that I got a beautiful wife like you. My friend Kartikeya revealed this secret to me."

The bride too decided to observe fasts on sixteen Mondays for a beautiful son full of knowledge. Her devotion bore fruit and she gave birth to a beautiful son. As the son grew up, he said to his mother, "O my dear mother, what is the mystery behind my birth? Please reveal it to me."

The mother told him how she observed Monday fasts. The son also decided to observe the fasts to gain a kingdom for his parents.

Incidentally, an old king's messengers from a nearby State came there in search of a beautiful and learned bridegroom for the princess. They proposed the princess' hand for him and he readily agreed. The king expired after sometime and the boy became the king.

The newly-made king continued his fasts for the next sixteen Mondays. On the seventeenth Monday, he arranged a large prayer party at a temple. All the arrangements were made well in advance. The king requested the queen to accompany him to the temple for breaking the fast after taking 'prasaad' from the priest. The queen refused to go with him. The king had to go alone. The king heard an oracle who echoed, "O king, turn out the queen from the palace or destruction will fall upon you."

The king returned to his palace. He summoned a conference of his ministers and told about the oracle. All of them were taken aback, as it was due to that princess that he became the king of the state. They agreed to his proposal only with a heavy heart. The queen was ultimately turned out.

The queen left the palace bare footed and in worn-out clothes. She was thirsty and fatigued. She met an old lady who had a load of spinned spindles on her head. She was going to the city. She felt pity on her and asked to help her in selling the yarn because she did not know the art of selling. The queen took that load on her head. Incidentally, strong wind blew away the spindles which disappeared in the dusty wind. The queen felt sorry and the old lady asked her to go away.

The queen went to an oilman's house and sought shelter. The oilman obliged her, but as she stepped in, all of his oil pots developed cracks and the oil began to flow on the ground. The oilman immediately turned her out.

The queen was now disheartened. She went to the bank of a river to quench her thirst. As she touched the water, the water dried up.

She then went to a deep jungle and saw a tank of water. As she went down the stairs and touched the crystal clear water, it became muddy. She cursed her fate and put a few drops of the muddy water in her mouth.

She was now tired and wanted to take rest under a shady tree. As she went near the tree its leaves began to fall and soon it became leafless. The cowherds saw this incident and told the whole story to the priest of a nearby temple. The priest called for the woman. He was surprised to see that the woman had royal features. He consoled her and provided her with all the facilities. But after some days, he also got fed up with her because whatever the woman touched became impure — may it be milk, food or water.

One day, the priest said, "O lady, what curse has fallen upon you? You reveal the mystery. The woman told him how she rejected a proposal to attend Monday fast prayer. The priest understood the whole thing. He knew it was Shiva's curse. He said, "O dear lady, you observe fasts on sixteen Mondays and Lord Shiva will absolve you of your sins.

The woman realised her mistake and observed the Monday fasts for sixteen Mondays. On the seventeenth Monday, the king said to himself, "My queen left my palace long ago. Her condition must be very miserable." He called for his courtiers and ordered them to search out the queen.

The courtiers reached the temple where the queen was residing. The priest refused to hand over the queen to them and said, "Let the king himself come to receive her."

The courtiers went to the king and related the whole story. The king was happy to hear the news. He went to the temple and requested the priest to return his queen to him. The king admitted that he deserted the queen to avoid Lord Shiva's wrath.

The priest trusted the king's words and the queen returned to the palace. She was given a royal welcome. The king distributed money among the needy and arranged food for the hungry.

The king and queen now regularly observed fasts on sixteen Mondays each year and lived a very happy life. After their death they found abode in Lord Shiva's city, Shivapuri.

Since, then it is believed that a person who observes fasts on sixteen Mondays, gets all pleasures and enters Shivapuri after his death.

3

Mangalvar Ki Kahani - I

(Mangal's Anguish)

(This story is listened to by those who observe Tuesday fast. They listen it before breaking the fast. The fast is observed for obtaining royal patronage, happiness or for getting a son. People generally wear red clothes at worship and offer red flowers to the deity. God Hanuman is also worshipped.)

Once there was a Brahman's son. He was married at an early age. He went to his father-in-law's village to get back his wife. His in-laws welcomed him heartily and gave him best dishes to eat. The boy said to his father-in-law, "Please send your daughter with me. My mother is unwell. There is nobody to look after her."

"That is correct," said the father-in-law, "but we have not made full preparations to offer her clothes and cash."

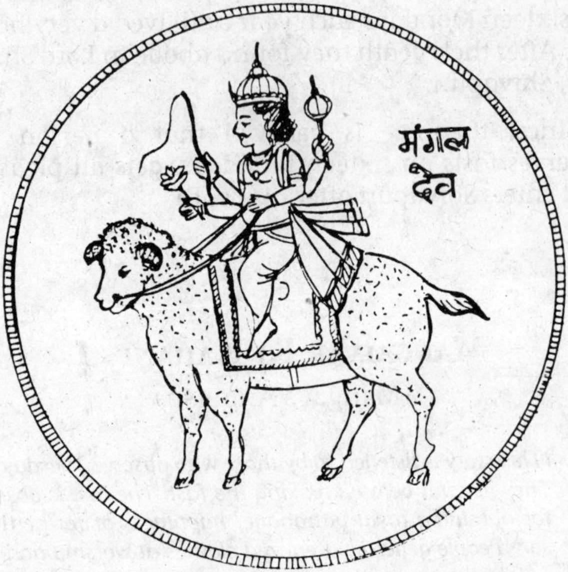

The boy said, "Our family is not so down-and-out as to accept such offers all the time. You send your daughter with me."

The boy's mother-in-law raised another objection and said, "My daughter is a newly-wed and she is very beautiful. She will wear gold ornaments. Who will guarantee her safety during the journey?"

The boy said, "I am brave enough to guard her. See my muscular body."

The mother-in-law said, "It is not the muscular body but the mind which guards us."

The boy said, "Do not consider me without mind." The father-in-law and the mother-in-law argued for some time with the son-in-law and finally agreed to send their daughter with him.

The young husband and wife both started their journey for the village. It was Tuesday. Tuesday is devoted to the god Mars. He is the commander of this day. The Mars saw the Brahman's beautiful wife. He was dazzled to see such a beauty. He knew witchcraft. He disguised himself as a Brahman's son and said to the boy," She is my wife. Who are you to accompany her? Give her to me, otherwise I will kill you."

The Brahman's son felt bewildered at the sight of an identical man like him. He said, "You are a ghost. You are a cheat. She is my wife. How can I give her to you?"

The woman would not differentiate between the two. She stood there puzzled. Some cow herds noticed their quarrel. They went to them and asked about the cause of their quarrel.

The Brahman's son said, "She is my wife. This man is a cheat. He wants to take away my wife under a false disguise. He is not the man who has married this woman. I am her real husband."

The Mars who was in the guise of Brahman's son said, "She is my wife and I am her real husband."

The cow-herds felt confused at their claims. One of the cow-herd asked the woman, "Who is your real husband?"

The lady said, "I was married when I was very young. I have cast my look at my husband for the first time, after long years. I cannot differentiate between the two."

The matter became still complicated. One of the cow-herds sensed the gravity of the situation. He could see that one of them was a spirit. He knew how to deal with such spirits.

He said, "Bring an earthen pot with a spout. I will hand over this lady to the real husband."

They arranged a Kuchcha *Karva* or a pot with a spout. The cowherd said, "This lady belongs to that person who can enter this pot through its spout."

The Brahman's son said, "This is injustice. I cannot enter this pot."

The cowherd said, "Then you are a cheat. You would have to abide by my order."

The Brahman's son kept mum. He was helpless.

The Mars said, "She is my wife. I can enter this pot through its spout."

The clever cowherd said, "If you enter this pot, she will be your wife."

The Mars was in the form of a spirit. He knew the craft of changing his body into any shape. He entered the pot through the spout. The cow-herd closed the spout with a tight cork. The Mars was imprisoned in the pot. He could not come out from it. To make his escape impossible, the cowherd dug a deep hole in the ground and put that earthen pot deep into it and filled the hole up.

The Brahman's son was happy. He thanked the cowherd for his intelligence and wisdom.

Since that day, it has been a belief that nobody should dig earth on Tuesday so that the devil spirit of the Mars remains inside the earth for ever.

Mangalvar Ki Kahani - II

(Mangalia)

(The devotees listen to this story before breaking Tuesday fast. Tuesday is devoted to Lord Hanuman. The devotees take saltless food and offer red sandal, red flowers and gur (jaggery) - mixed food to the deity. Plastering houses with cow dung is forbidden on this day. Vermillon mark is made on the forehead.)

Once there lived an old lady. She worshipped her favourite deity, Mangal or Mars with full devotion. She kept fast on Tuesdays to propitiate the Mars.

The lady had a son. His name was Mangal. He was incidentally born on Tuesday. She called him Mangalia out of love.

The lady never plastered her house with cowdung on Tuesdays and never dug earth on this auspicious day.

Once Lord Mars came to her house to fathom her faith in him. He was disguised as a sadhu. He knocked at the old woman's door. The woman came out and said, "What can I do for you?"

The sadhu said, "I am very hungry. I want to cook food for myself. Please besmear some portion of your kitchen to make room for my cooking. I shall be thankful to you."

The old lady said, "My Lord, I am on Tuesday fast. So I cannot besmear the kitchen. If you permit me I shall sprinkle some fresh water on the spot where you want to do cooking. You may cook your meals there."

The sadhu said, "I cook my food only on a besmeared spot." The old lady said, "Please let me know anything other than besmearing the kitchen. I am ready to do it."

The sadhu said, "Think thrice before you commit me a task. You will have to carry out my command."

The old lady said again, "My Lord, I shall abide by all your orders except for besmearing the spot."

The sadhu said, "Send for your son. Ask him to lie down on the ground. I will cook my meals upon your son's back."

The old lady was stunned to hear the sadhu's words. She kept mum. The sadhu said, "You have given me a word. Call your son immediately. Do not give further thought to your words."

The old woman called out for her son, "O! Mangalia, O! dear Mangalia, come immediately. Serve the sadhu. Abide by his commands because I have given him a word."

The son was playing in a nearby lane. He heard his mother's call. He came running and asked for her orders.

The old lady said, "Go to that sadhu and obey his orders."

The boy went to the sadhu and said, "I am at your command. Order me."

The sadhu said, "Go and come with your mother."

The old lady came to the sadhu. The sadhu said, "Help your son lie down on the ground."

The old lady brought image of Lord Mars before her mind's eyes and made her son lie up side down on the ground. She then placed the hearth on her son's back with her own hands and, said, "My Lord, cook your meals as you like. I am going to do some other household work."

The sadhu lit the hearth on the boy's back and cooked his meals.

When the meals were ready, the sadhu said to the old lady, "Give a call to your son. Let him have his share of meals."

The old lady said, "This is a wonder. You cooked your food on his back. How can he be called now? Is it possible that he is alive? Please do not ask me to think of him again. Take this food yourself and bid goodbye to this house."

The sadhu insisted that the lady should call her son for taking his share of food as a blessing from him. The old lady agreed and said, "Oh! Mangalia, dear Mangalia, this sadhu wants to offer you some part of food he cooked on your back. Come wherever you are."

The old lady had hardly called her son when Mangal came running. The sadhu gave him some food as a token of his blessings. He then said to the lady, "Your Tuesday fast has attained perfection. It has borne fruit. You are a kind lady. You have unshakable faith in your favourite deity. You will never face any difficulty in your life."

Mangalvar Ki Kahani - III

(Hanuman's Kindness)

(Tuesday is devoted to Lord Hanuman. The devotees listen to this story before breaking their fast in the afternoon. The wrestlers do not massage their bodies on this day to avoid hairfalling. Some wrestlers observe Tuesday as a rest day.)

Once there was an old lady. She used to observe Tuesday fast. She enjoyed all sorts of prosperity. Her daughter-in-law used to give her four loaves on every Tuesday. She used to go to the Hanuman Temple and offered two loaves there. The remaining two she ate herself and felt satisfied.

Once the daughter-in-law asked her children to follow their grandmother and to keep a watch over her activities. Her grandsons noticed that their grandmother offered two loaves to Lord Hanuman and broke her fast with the remaining two. They reported the matter to their mother. Their mother thought that the old lady was wasting two loaves and decided to cook two loaves only.

On the next Tuesday, the daughter-in-law gave her only two loaves. The old lady went to the Hanuman temple and offered one loaf to Hanuman and broke her fast with the remaining one. Her grandsons noticed her and reported the matter to their mother. Their mother thought that the old lady was wasting one loaf and decided to give her one loaf only.

The old lady accepted one loaf on the coming Tuesday and went to the Hanuman temple. She offered half a loaf to lord Hanuman and broke her fast with the other half. Her grandson noticed it and reported again to their mother. Their mother thought that the old lady was wasting her food at family's expense. She decided not to give her any loaf on Tuesdays.

The old lady went to the Hanuman temple empty-handed. She had nothing to offer. Lord Hanuman appeared before her as a young boy and said, "O, old ma, what ails you?"

The old lady related the whole story to the young boy. The young boy said, "Why don't you erect a cottage of yours behind this temple? Take me as your son. I shall arrange food for you. What is the use of living with a family which does not care for its elders!"

The old lady agreed and started living in the cottage. Everyday the young boy would bring a mug full of milk and a lump of crushed bread mixed with sugar and butter (churma) for her. Her life was now very happy and peaceful.

The old lady's daughter-in-law became poorer and poorer day-after-day. Unwanted quarrels broke out in the house due to poverty. They had little to eat. One day she said to her children, "Go to your grandmother and observe what she does."

The children went to their grandmother. The old lady welcomed them. She shared milk and 'Churma' with them and asked them to visit her everyday.

The children went back to their house and related the whole thing to their mother. She was surprised to know that the old lady was hale and hearty instead of growing weak. She realised her mistake and asked her husband to bring her back.

Her husband said, "Why should I go? You are responsible for our sufferings. You make quarrels in the family everyday. You forced her to leave this house. You were jealous of her even for meager meals. This house lost its prosperity the moment she left us. You have no regards for your elders and their noble deeds."

The lady said, "Let all of us go to her. We shall convince her that she should come back."

Her husband agreed and they went to the old lady. The young boy was sitting with her and serving her food. The old lady's daughter-in-law fell at the feet of her mother-in-law and begged pardon of her for her misdeeds.

The old lady said to the young boy; "Should I accompany them as they have realised their mistake?" The young boy said, "Yes, you may. If you face any difficulty, you may come back."

The old lady returned to her family. She observed Tuesday fasts and her daughter-in-law never objected to her giving half of her food to Lord Hanuman. Prosperity again visited their house and they lived a happy life.

Mangalvar Ki Kahani - IV

(The Suspicious Brahman)

(Unwanted suspicion, doubt or misbelief creates unhappiness in the family. Unshakeable faith in one god brings happiness. A chaste life is above suspicion.)

Once there lived a Brahman couple. They were issueless. So their life was very unhappy. The Brahman went to the jungles to appease Lord Hanuman. He would pray for a child in his prayers. His wife used to observe fasts on Tuesdays to placate the Lord. She used to take her food on Mondays only after offering 'Prasaad' to Lord Hanuman.

Once she observed some special fast for the whole day. So she could not offer 'Prasaad' to Hanuman. She was very sorry for it and felt guilty. She decided to observe a fast till the coming Tuesday. She said to herself that she would take her meals only after offering 'Prasaad' to Hanuman.

She became weak and fragile and even fainted due to the long fast. Hanuman took pity on her and appeared before her in the guise of a child. Hanuman said, "I bless you with a beautiful son. He will always serve you, day and night." He then disappeared after blessing the lady.

Fortunately, the lady got a beautiful son. She named him Mangal. The Brahman returned home after some months. He saw a handsome child playing in his courtyard. He became suspicious and said to his wife, "Whose child is this? Have you indulged in adultery?"

The woman said politely, "My dear husband, I am a chaste lady. I used to observe Tuesday fast in your absence to please Lord Hanuman. He has blessed me with this child. Please believe me."

The Brahman kept mum but deep in his heart, doubts began to curl up every moment. The lady was helpless.

One day the Brahman was going to take his bath at some nearby well. The lady told him, "Please take Mangal alongwith you. He is quite grown-up. He will fetch water for your bath. He will also rub your back."

The Brahman agreed and took the boy alongwith him. He thought it would be a good occasion to push him into the well and to get-rid of a sinful child for good.

As the boy was to fetch water, the Brahman pushed the boy into the well and returned home.

To her great surprise, the woman noticed that the Brahman did not have wet *dhoti* on his shoulders. She said, "Have you taken your bath?" The Brahman said, "Yes."

The lady said, "Please give me your wet 'dhoti' to enable me to spread it on the string."

The Brahman was nonplussed. He had guilty conscience. He murmured some words and tried to leave the house. The wife said, "Where is my Mangal? Where is my Mangal? O! Mangal, appear before my eyes if I am a cheste lady and you are my true son."

To the great surprise of both the wife and the husband, Mangal appeared at the door. He embraced his mother and touched his father's feet.

That might Lord Hanuman appeared before the Brahman in his dreams and said, "O! poor creature, I blessed you with a son, and you suspect your wife of adultery. You must feel sorry for it."

The Brahman realised his mistake. His wife regularly observed fasts on Tuesdays. Thereafter they led a happy life. It is said that whosoever reads or listens to this story and keeps regular fasts Lord Hanuman protects him from all evils and bestows all happiness.

4
Budhvar Ki Kahani

(The devotees who keep the fast on Wednesdays take their meals once a day, generally in the afternoon. The use of green articles is preferred. The fast is observed in the name of Lord Shiva. It is believed that it promotes happiness in life and deepens love between husband and wife. The devotees listen to this story before breaking the fast. Wednesday is also connected with Planet Mercury.)

Once there was a newly-wed. On a Sunday, he went to his father-in-law's house to take his wife with him. It was the first time after marriage.

He was welcomed by the in-laws and was provided with best food and bedding. His wife's friends cut jokes with him. He enjoyed their jokes and conversation. He forgot the outside world as he enjoyed the hospitality offered to him by his wife's younger brothers and sisters.

Monday and Tuesday were spent in other pastimes. It was now Wednesday. He told his mother-in-law, "I have an urgent piece of work today. You send your daughter with me immediately."

"But today is Wednesday. Mercury is not favourable to girls on Wednesday. It is considered inauspicious sending daughters in their in-laws' house. I shall not send my daughter today," said the mother-in-law."

"I care a fig for the Mercury. He cannot harm me. Wednesday is very favourable for the businessmen like me. I have also very urgent piece of work at home," said the son-in-law.

The mother-in-law said, "You came here on Sunday. Monday was your hospitality day. The guest should enjoy only one day's hospitality. You have over-stayed. This is not our fault. How could we ask you to go away on Tuesday? It was for you to decide. Now, please go tomorrow for heaven's sake."

The son-in-law was adamant. He insisted on leaving the same day. The in-laws read his mood and agreed to send their daughter with him.

They arranged a chariot for the couple. Soon, the couple reached near a township. The girl was thirsty. She said to her husband, "I am very thirsty. Please arrange some cold water for me."

The husband agreed and went towards the township. Another youngman resembling her husband brought water for her. She could not distinguish between the two. She took him for her husband and had a good chat with him.

In the meanwhile, her real husband appeared on the scene. He was surprised to see his wife chatting and cutting jokes with someone else. He was annoyed at her conduct. The wife also felt bemused when she saw the like of her husband standing with a water pot in his hand.

Both the males quarrelled among themselves and claimed the lady as their wife. Incidentally a constable came there and wanted to know what the matter was. He said to the lady, "Who is your real husband?"

The lady said, "I am in a fix myself. They resemble each other so much."

The real husband felt sorry. He remembered his mother-in-law's words.

The constable took them to the king and told the whole story. The king asked his minister to administer justice.

The minister said to the constable, "It is late evening. Lock them up in separate cells. Arrange strict night watch. I will give my judgement tomorrow."

All the three were locked up in separate cells. It was dead of night. Mercury had a sound sleep. The real husband was very restless. He was repentant. He uttered loudly, "I am suffering for my pride and disobedience to my in-laws. Oh God, forgive me this time."

The guards were marking all these utterings. The next morning the minister sent for the guards. The guards related one of the youngmen's behaviour.

The minister said, "The man who had a restless night is the real husband. His wife should be restored to him. He should be freed. Produce the second person in my court."

The guards went to the prison cell. They set free the real husband and his wife. They were happy to be together again.

The guards went to the other youngman. His cell was empty though locked from outside. They reported the matter to the minister. He was astonished to know that the cell was empty though locked from outside. He went to the senior minister and related the whole story.

The senior minister smiled and said, "The missing prisoner is Mercury. Mercury rules on Wednesdays. This man challenged Mercury's authority. He felt offended and disguised himself as her husband to teach him a lesson. Today is Thursday. Jupiter rules on Thursdays. Mercury disappeared exactly at sunrise. Don't be afraid. The guards are not at fault."

The king was happy over his minister's judgement. The husband and wife reached home and related the whole story to their near and dear ones.

5
VRIHASPATIVAR KI KAHANI - I

(This story is connected with Thursday Fast. Devotees listen this story before breaking their fast. They also worship Vrihaspati Mahadeva or Jupiter. They wear yellow clothes and shower yellow flowers. Meals with yellow colour are preferred. Women worship the banana tree and water it. Food items are made with yellow-coloured cow's ghee.)

Once there was a rich man. He had a big palace. His wife was always busy with household matters.

One day a sadhu came to his house. The rich man was away. His wife was busy with some work. The sadhu said, "O, kind lady, I am hungry. Will you give me something to eat?"

The lady said, "Today is Thursday. I am busy cleaning my courtyard. Come on some other day when I am free."

The sadhu went away empty-handed. He visited her house again on another day and said, "O, kind lady, I am hungry. Will you give me something to eat?" The lady was a miser. She said, "I am arranging bath for my grandson. I am not free. Come on some other day."

The sadhu again went away empty-handed. He visited her house again for the third time. She repeated her words and said, "You always visit when I am busy. You are not a wise sadhu."

The sadhu said humbly, "Will you give me something to eat if you are free on some day?"

The lady answered, "I will definitely give you something to eat if I am free. The problem with me is that I am never free. Is there some way out for me? Tell me the way."

The sadhu smiled and said, "Yes, there is a way out." "What's it?" asked the lady.

The sadhu said, "Get up late on every Thursday morning. Do not clean your kitchen before cooking meals. Put the cooked meals behind the hearth. Wash your hair and clothes on every Thursday. Ask your husband to get himself shaved on this day."

The sadhu disappeared and the lady followed his instructions. The rich man's family became poorer and poorer. They could hardly afford meals for one time.

The sadhu came again and said, "O, kind lady, I am hungry. Will you give me something to eat?" The lady said, "I am very poor these days. I have nothing to spare for you. I have nothing to do throughout the day".

"But when I visited you last, you were very busy. You gave me nothing to eat under the pretext that you would give me something when you were not busy. Today you are free, still you are not giving me anything. I doubt your intentions," said the sadhu and he disappeared.

The lady said to her husband, "We are in great difficulty. Think of something for the livelihood."

The man said, "It is better to beg outside one's land rather than take resort to robbery or stealing. I shall go to some far off place for business."

The lady agreed. Before departure, the man advised his wife, saying, "Always keep the water pitcher full of water. It should never be empty. Let the hearth-fire burn day and night. It should never be put out."

And with these words, the businessman left his house. The lady tried to follow her husband's advice.

Incidentally, one day the hearth-fire got extinguished. The lady felt sorry and asked her maid to go to the neighbourhood and fetch some charcoal fire. The maid went to the neighbourhood but returned very late. The lady said, "Why are you so late? I have been waiting for you all along."

The maid begged pardon and said, "Our neighbour is a rich lady. She keeps fast on every Thursday and listens to Thursday's story. I joined her and listened to the story. Please excuse me for being late."

The lady said, "I also used to keep fast on Thursdays. We, too, were very rich those days. Hence onward, I shall also observe this fast."

The lady observed Thursday fast continuously for seven weeks. She wore yellow saree, took some gram pulse on her palm and listened to the story of Vrihaspati. Vrihaspati was pleased with her devotion. He appeared before her as a sadhu and said, "Lord Vrihaspati wants to oblige you. You can ask for any favour."

The lady said, "I am very poor. Let our wealth and property be restored to us."

The sadhu said, "Let it be!" and he disappeared immediately.

The lady continued with the Thursday fasts for another seven weeks. The sadhu again appeared on the seventh Thursday and said, "O, gentle devotee, Lord Vrihaspati is pleased with your devotion. He wants to oblige you. You can ask for any other favour. He will fulfil your desire."

The lady said, "Lord Vrihaspati has restored our wealth and property. But these possessions are useless without my husband."

The sadhu said, "Your husband will return soon" and he disappeared. The businessman had a dream. Some sadhu said to him, "You are rich now. Your wife is waiting for your happy return." The businessman woke up and decided to return home. He was at a far off place and it took him a couple of months to reach home.

When the businessman neared his village, he enquired about his wife's well-being from women fetching water from the village well. One of them said, "Your wife is enjoying a happy and rich life. A sadhu visits her house every Thursday. He is very kind to her."

The businessman got suspicious about his wife's fidelity. Incidentally, it was Thursday. He thought of keeping a watch on her. When he reached his house, a sadhu came out of the door. The businessman caught hold of him and said, "Who are you? Why do you visit my wife in my absence? I will kill you."

The sadhu said nothing but simply smiled. In the meanwhile, his wife also came out and said, "Please do not kill him. He has helped me during our days of trial."

The businessman got more suspicious. He pulled out his sword and attacked the sadhu. To his great surprise, his sword turned into a wooden one. For a few seconds, he stood bemused, but soon realised his mistake. He fell on the sadhu's feet and begged his pardon. He also came to know that the sadhu was no one else but Lord Vrihaspati himself.

Thereafter, the husband and wife observed Thursday fast regularly and for a long time lived a happy life.

Vrihaspativar Ki Kahani - II

(Banana's Goddess)

Once there was a young girl. She used to water a banana tree. She also used to play under it. One day a strange voice came as if fluttering from its leaves. The girl got frightened and ran away.

Next day the girl was again watering the tree. She heard the same voice. She took courage. The voice said, "Will you play with me? Will you play with me?"

The young girl looked here and there. She could locate nobody there. She started to grow weaker and weaker. Her mother noted this change. One day the mother said, "My dear girl, what is wrong with you? Why are you losing your health despite best food?"

The young girl said, "I water my banana tree everyday. I hear a strange voice from it. The voice says 'Will you please play with me?' I see no one around me."

The mother heard her daughter and said smilingly, "You are a very innocent girl. The banana goddess is pleased with you. You welcome her tomorrow for playing."

The girl heard the same voice the next day. She invited her to play with her. After the play was over, the goddess of banana or Lakshmi said to the girl, "Will you please accompany me to my house for lunch?"

The girl said, "Have you a house too?"

The goddess took her to her palace through the hollow of the banana tree and served her with best sweets and fruit in gold and silver pots. She offered her various types of costly gifts. When the girl returned, her mother was happy. She said to her daughter, "Have you offered your friend a return visit? You must invite her next day."

The girl said, "We are very poor. How can I extend invitation to her? Our utensils are broken. Our clothes are shabby and torn. We have nothing to sit upon."

The mother said, "Service and courtesy will compensate for them. We will clean our house and give her a warm welcome."

The girl agreed to her mother's advice. When she met the goddess the next day, she extended to her invitation for visiting her house. The goddess accepted the invitation. She accompanied the girl to her house the next day.

The goddess had hardly stepped into the house when it was converted into a beautiful palace. The broken utensils turned into shining gold and silver ones. The shabby and torn clothes became new and attractive. The ordinary meal prepared by the family tasted like mana.

As she was about to leave, the goddess blessed the family with a happy future. The girl's mother requested the goddess to stay with them permanently.

The goddess said, "I am goddess Lakshmi. I am of very unstable and fickle-minded. I cannot commit to stay with you all the time. So long as you work hard and water the banana trees, I shall be there in form of banana fruit. Your business will flourish day by day. Water banana tree, especially on Thursdays."

The goddess then disappeared from the scene leaving plenty of wealth for the family.

VRIHASPATIVAR KI KAHANI - III

(Vrihaspati Saved Indra)

(Showing discourtesy or disgrace to guru brings sufferings and sorrows. One's heinous deeds affect society.)

Once Lord Indra, surrounded by many gods, Rishis, Kinnaras and Gandharvas sat on his throne in a proudy mood. As guru Vrihaspati reached there all of them except Indra stood up to pay respect. Indra used to pay obedience to his guru regularly but he showed discourtesy at that time. Vrihaspati felt bad and left his palace. As Vrihaspati left the palace Lord Indra realised his mistake and repented over his action. He felt that all his luxurious possessions were due to his guru's blessings. Guru's anger will turn it to dust.

Indra decided to go to Vrihaspati and tender apology for his action. It may pacify his anger. He went to Vrihaspati. Vrihaspati intuited that Indra was coming to his Ashram. He avoided meeting out of anger and disappeared immediately. Lord Indra returned home disappointed.

A demon god Vrishvarsha, sensed this situation and went to his guru Shukracharya. He begged his guru's permission to attack Indrapuri, the kingdom of Lord Indra in those circumstances. Shukracharya permitted him. The demon god surrounded Indrapuri and made a sudden attack. In the absence of Guru Vrihaspati's blessings the gods lost all battles one after the other.

After his defeat the gods went to Lord Brahma and related the whole story. He begged for safety and asked for some strategy. Lord Brahma said, "You have not done good by disgracing Vrihaspati. Anyway go to Vishwaroopa the learned son of Twashta. Request him to become your priest. His blessings can save you."

They went to Twashta and sought his blessings. Twashta said, "By becoming your priest I do not want to lessen my virtues. But you go to my son Vishwaroopa. He will oblige you by accepting your request for priesthood."

All the gods went to Vishwaroopa and requested him to become their family priest for perfoming Yajna. He accepted their request. By Vishwaroopa's grace demon Vrishvarsha was defeated and Lord Indra regained his kingdom.

Lord Indra was happy. He implored Vishwaroopa to perform a special 'yajna' for further gains. Vishwaroopa agreed. Vishwaroopa had three mouths. With one mouth he sucked the juice of 'Sompalli' a special creeper. From the second mouth he used to drink wine. He used his third mouth for eating meals.

Vishwaroopa started performing Yajna. The demon gods were frightened. They thought a plan to undo the Yajna's effects. One of the demon god went to Vishwaroopa and implored, "Honourable Sir, do you know that you belong to demon genealogy from your mother's side. Your mother is the daughter of a demon god. While performing Yajna kindly make some offerings in the names of demon gods for their happiness. Vishwaroopa agreed to his request. He made some silent offerings to demon gods so that no one may hear it. The result was that the Yajna's advantages were divided between dieties and demon gods.

When Lord Indra came to know the treachery he beheaded Vishwaroopa in a state of extreme anger. One of his mouth from which he took wine, turned into a black bee. The second which he used for sucking 'Sompalli' juice became a piglion while the third one used for taking meals was transformed into a partridge.

Lord Indra's body was immediately deformed due to sacrelige, the murder of a Brahman. All the gods made repentance for one year but it had no effect on Indra. They approached Lord Brahma for seeking some remedy to redeem Indra from the sacrelige. Lord Brahma accompanied by Vrihaspati went to Indra. He decided the sacrelige act into four parts.

The first part was given to the earth. As a result the earth became uneven. Some of its portion became barren. But as a boon he said that the earth would develop power to fill the 'khuds' automatically.

The second part of the sacrelige was given to the trees and as a result they began to ooze gum. But as a boon he said that the gum of 'guggul' - bdellium olibanum - will be treated pure and they would have the power to rebud from their roots though their upper portion may be dried up.

The third part of the sacrelige was given to the woman folk and so they experience menstruation. As a boon he blessed them to the pure or chaste on the fourth day and capable to give birth to children.

The fourth portion of the sacrelige was given to water. As a result it is covered with aquatic plant or 'Shaivaal'. As a boon the object in which it is added gains weight.

In this way Lord Brahma freed Indra from the henious crime by dividing it into four places. Who so ever reads or listens this story is blessed by Vrihaspati.

6

SHUKRAVAR KI KAHANI- I

(Impact of Venus Planet)

(This story is related with Friday. The devotees wear white clothes on this day and eat white food, like kheer, only once at night. Sour dishes are avoided. It is believed that all the afflictions due to Shukra get pacified if one keeps a fast on this day. One gets all sorts of joys and happiness. Shukra is Venus Planet. Shukra's idol is worshipped with white flowers and rice.)

In good old days, there lived three friends. They belonged to Brahman, Baniya and royal families. They were fast friends. All the three were married but the Baniya's son had not brought home his wife after his marriage ceremony.

One day, the three friends were together gossiping. They talked about their wives. The Brahman's son and the prince praised their wives and said, "A home without a wife is a devil's abode."

They asked the Baniya's son to bring his wife as soon as he could.

The Baniya's son went to his house and said to his mother, "I will go to my in-laws to bring back my wife."

His mother said, "My dear son, the Venus Planet is still set. It is not visible in the sky. Wait for a couple of days. Venus is the planet of love. If you go and bring back your wife now, your married life may not be happy."

The son did not agree and insisted on going to his in-laws. The parents permitted reluctantly. The young Baniya reached his in-laws house and told them about his mission. His in-laws said, "The planet Venus is still setting. It will be visible after a couple of days. Parents do not send away their daughters during this period. It is inauspicious."

The boy did not agree. The parents parted with their daughter reluctantly. The couple had hardly crossed the town when the wheel of their bullock cart got damaged. The bullock's legs were also injured. The young lady was badly wounded. Still, the youngman continued the journey despite all the adversities.

As they went ahead, they encountered some dacoits. The dacoits robbed the bride of her ornaments and beat up her husband. At last, they reached home after facing many set-backs. The youngman was also bitten by a poisonous snake and he became unconscious. The young wife wept bitterly.

The Brahman's son came to know of the incident. He went to his friend's house and said to his father, "Arrange return journey for them. They should not have started their journey during the forbidden period. The Venus is invisible in the sky. They will be out of danger if they go back to the in-laws."

The businessman arranged their return journey. When the youngman reached his in-laws' house, he came back to himself and recovered from his illness after an ordinary treatment. He stayed there till the Venus became visible in the horizon. Afterwards, he returned to his house with his wife and lived a happy life. He started observing Friday fast regularly thereafter.

Shukravar Ki Kahani- II

(Shukra's Idol)

Once there was an old woman. She used to observe Friday fasts regularly. She worshipped Shukra's idol. She gave holy dips to the idol and offered best food to it as 'bhoga'.

One day she decided to go on a pilgrimage. But how could she leave the house? Who would give holy dips to Shukra's idol? Who would offer 'bhoga' to it?

She conveyed her anxiety to her son's wife. Her son's wife, that is her daughter-in-law was not a religious lady. She wanted to get rid of her mother-in-law for some time. She agreed to worship Shukra's idol in her absence.

The old lady felt happy and left on the pilgrimage. Her daughter-in-law being what she was, after taking her bath would squeeze a few drops of water from her wet saree and considered it as a dip for the idol. She would prepare best dishes in her mother-in-law's absence and place some crumbs or remains before the idol as 'bhoga'. Even this was heavy for her.

One day she decided to get rid of the idol. She put it in a waste paper basket and threw it on a heap of garbage.

A wise lady passed by. She noticed Shukra's bright idol lying on the garbage. She picked it up with great respect and brought it to her house. She gave it holy dips and offered best 'bhoga'. She also observed fast in the name of Shukra. The lady became very rich. On the other hand, the old woman's family became poorer and poorer. The family could hardly make both ends meet.

The old lady returned from her pilgrimage. She noticed the changed conditions of the family. She asked the daughter-in-law, "Where is the Shukra's idol?" The daughter-in-law kept mum. She repeated the question, but the lady would not speak. She repeated her question, for the third time. The daughter-in-law replied, "I was fed up with Shukra's worship. I had no time to spare. I threw it on a heap of garbage some weeks ago."

The old lady was astonished at the reply. She went to the garbage heap and searched for the idol, but had to return disappointed. She decided to go from door to door to enquire about it.

She knocked at the door of a rich lady and said, "Have you seen my Shukra's idol?"

The rich lady gazed at her from head to foot and said, "Are you insane? Why did you throw the idol on the garbage? You have no regards for deities. You should be punished for it."

The old lady narrated the whole story to the rich lady and felt sorry for her daughter-in-law. The rich lady said, "If it is so I shall return the idol to you". Lord Shukra has blessed me with health and wealth. I do not want to keep others' things with me. Take back this idol with full respect."

The old lady brought back the idol and placed it at the worshipping dias. She observed Shukra's fasts as a penance. Lord Shukra again blessed them with health and wealth. The family enjoyed a happy life again thereafter.

7
Shanivar Ki Kahani- I

(This story is related to Saturday fast. The devotees worship Saturn idol made of iron. Black flowers, black sesame seeds (tils), horse bean (urada) and black clothes are used for worship. Black articles and oil are given in donation. Black sesame and horse bean are taken as food. Wives do not perform journey to their paternal home town. The Saturday fast keeps away all the hurdles and misfortunes. Saturn sits in a mirror chariot, yoked with eight black horses.)

Once there was a Brahman. He used to guard against evil spirits at the king's main gate palace.

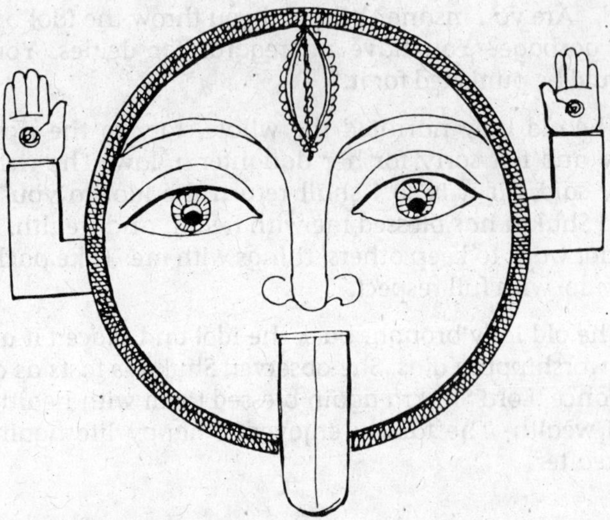

One day he heard a strange voice and was frightened. He heard this voice for a number of days. He never talked about that mysterious voice to his wife.

One day his wife said, "I try to provide you best nutritious meals, still you are losing your health. What is wrong with you?"

For some time, he kept mum. His wife insisted that he should reveal his internal feelings to get rid of any unnecessary strain. The Brahman said, "I hear a strange voice every Saturday. It says that it wants to afflict the king. The duration of affliction will be either seven-and-a-half years or two-and-a-half years or two-and-a-half months or two-and-a-half days or at least for two-and-a-half *prahar* i.e. seven-and-a-half hours. The king can opt for any period but the affliction is a must."

The Brahman's wife smiled and said, "Why didn't you tell it earlier? The king must be saved even at our cost. You accept two-and-a-half *'prahars'* affliction for you."

The spirit again visited the palace and repeated the same message. The Brahman said, "I offer to take King's affliction upon myself. You can be upon me for two-and-a-half *prahars.*"

The spirit was pleased at Brahman's offer.

The Brahman went to a riverbank. He wanted to spent that time in meditation. He noticed two water-melons floating on the surface of water. He caught them by their tops and placed them under his thigh.

The king's princes had been out for hunting for the last two days. They had not returned. The king was in great agony. He sent his messengers in various directions for searching out the princes.

Incidentally, a messenger came to the Brahman. To his great surprise, he saw that the Brahman was hiding the heads of the princes under his thigh.

He reported the matter to the king. The king was enraged. He ordered that the Brahman be impaled or hanged.

The king asked the Brahman what his last desire was. The Brahman said, "Please do not kill me for two-and-a-half *prahars.*"

The king agreed. As the stipulated time was over arrangements for Brahman's end were made ready. The Brahman was to be beheaded with a red hot iron spear. As the slaughter man attacked the Brahman, the hot spear got broken into pieces. The slaughter man now took a red hot silver spear. That spear too was broken into pieces before it touched the Brahman's neck. The slaughter man took out a red hot golden spear and tried to behead the Brahman. The third spear also did have a different fate.

The onlookers were surprised at the sight of such a miracle. Suddenly, the princes too, appeared at the scene. The king embraced the princes and felt sorry for the Brahman.

The king said, "O, Brahman! What is this puzzle?" Reveal this mystery to one and all."

The Brahman said, "The Saturn wanted to afflict you. I took your affliction upon me to save you and the kingdom. The Saturn made the water melons appear as human heads. Now could I have killed the princes? I have always been a saviour of this kingdom." The king said, "I don't believe your utterings. I want to see the Saturn myself. If you do not show me, all the members of your family will be crushed in the grinder."

The Brahman began to tremble. He begged for a week's time. He went to his house. His wife said, "You look pale and horrified. What is the matter?" The Brahman said, "The Saturn wrought the affliction on me. I was saved because I acted according to your advice. Now, if I do not show Saturn to the king, all of us will be crushed under the grinder wheels."

The Brahman's wife said, "Have patience. You staked your life for a better cause. God will help us."

The Brahman had a sigh of relief. His wife said, "Ask the king to get up early in the morning on the coming Saturday. Saturn will be riding a black horse under the black mountain. He will be covered with a black blanket, all soaked in oil. The king can have his glimpse."

The Brahman took the king to the black mountain the next Saturday. A black shadow was riding a black horse. The king said, "Who are you?" The Saturn said, "I am Saturn. I afflict the poor as well as the kings alike."

The king said, "How can we avoid your affliction?" The Saturn said, "The rich should donate a black horse or one-and-a-quarter maunds of gold on Saturday. The middle-income group can donate iron and black blankets. The poor can give oil-touched loaf to a black dog. The still poorer can water a peepal tree, place some *gur* there and wrap the tree with a piece of *kuchcha* thread."

The Brahman said, "Do not afflict our king. Your affliction on the king will affect our town. I can stand your afflictions on myself in the future also."

The Saturn suddenly disappeared alongwith his black horse and the king returned to his palace. He was pleased with the Brahman.

The Brahman's wife felt happy when the husband reported the whole happening to her.

Shanivar Ki Kahani- II

(Shani's Affliction)

(This story is also related to Saturday fast. People eat parched grams on this day to keep off the influence of Saturn. They massage their bodies with mustard oil and also give oil in donation.)

Once the seven gods, the lords of the seven days of the week, were having exchange of wit for their amusement. Rahu and Ketu also joined the company. Rahu and Ketu posed a question—who is the most powerful god among us all? They could not decide this issue by themselves. They went to Lord Indra for his adjudication.

Lord Indra equally found himself in a fix. He thought if he gave judgement in favour of one, others would be displeased with him. He said, "Respected gods, I am just one among equals. How can I decide this complicated issue? I cannot give an impartial judgement. Better go to planet earth. Vir Vikramaditya rules over there. He is very logical, judicious and righteous. Accordingly, they went to King Vikramaditya.

King Vikramaditya gave due respect to them and begged for any service. They told him about their mission. Though it was a difficult task, Vikramaditya being a dutiful king, accepted it gracefully. Vikramaditya decided that he would not pronounce his verdict directly. He, therefore arranged seven beautiful thrones. These thrones were made of gold, silver, bronze, brass, tin, zinc, mica and iron respectively. The gold throne was placed at number one and the iron one at the end. Vikramaditya requested the seven gods to grace the throne of their own choice. Sun was in the gold chair while Saturn occupied the iron chair.

When the seven gods were in the chairs of their own choice, king Vikramaditya said, "You may please decide your own rank now according to the order to your throne. I have not thrust my judgement upon you."

Saturn could see now through the clever judgement of Vikramaditya. He stood up and said, "King Vikramaditya, you have ranked me the lowest among the seven gods. You do not realise my power. Sun can stay on a zodiac or 'Rashi' for one month and two and a quarter part of a day, Mars for one and a half months and Jupitor for thirteen months. Mercury and Venus can reign a zodiac for one month only. The Rahu and Ketu move in opposite directions and pass through a zodiac in eighteen months only. It is only I who can reign a zodiac from two and a half years to seven and a half years. Even powerful gods tremble at my sight. When I was angry with Rama, he got exile instead of a throne. Ravana's family was destroyed by me when I ruled over his zodiac. Now be prepared. It is your turn."

After a short time, inauspicious period of seven and a half years was occupied by Saturn on king Vikramaditya's zodiac. He visited Vikramaditya's capital as a horse trader. He had very attractive black horses with him. When the king came to know about the strange horses, he sent for the Ashavapaal (groom) to buy a best horse for him. The groom selected one horse.

The king was so pleased to see the horse. He could not resist himself from riding it and giving it a kick. He had hardly gone on the horse for a few seconds when it disappeared in the air with a great speed. In no time, the king found himself all alone in a deep and thick forest. He loitered here and there, but of no avail. He then met a cowboy. The cowboy arranged some water for the king and helped him quench his thirst. The king gave him his golden ring.

The king ultimately reached a nearby city and met a respectable businessman. The businessman felt pity on him and arranged food for him. He earned high profits by the grace of Saturn and took 'king' as a lucky visitor and kept him as a head cashier.

Next day the businessman took him to his house. The 'king' saw a precious necklace hanging by a peg. For his great surprise he also saw the peg swallowing the necklace. He could not explain it to the businessman. The businessman took him for a thief and presented him before the court. The court ordered that the king's hands and feet be cut with one stroke of a sword. An executor carried out these orders.

The 'king' was now without hands and feet. A 'Teli' (oil seed crusher) felt pity on him and brought him to his house. He dressed the 'king's' wounds and made him capable of driving the bullocks around the grinding machine with loud voice.

Time passed on. The inauspicious period of seven and a half years was about to be over. The 'king' thought of singing the Malhar Raga on a rainy day. His powerful voice broke the silence of the night. The princess was thrilled to hear the song in her bedroom. She got fascinated towards the singer.

The princess sent her personal attendant to know about the singer. The attendant was told that the singer was a help to the Teli and without hands and feet. Even then she decided that she would marry that man or would remain unmarried throughout her life. She conveyed her decision to her parents. The parents resented the decision. To register her protest, she put on ordinary clothes and moved to a special chamber or Kopa Bhawan and lay down on an ordinary carpet. The king and the queen ultimately bowed before the princess's decision and said, "If such is your fate, we are reconciled to it."

The king sent for the Teli and said, "Arrange for the marriage of this handicapped help of yours with the princess."

The Teli did not believe his ears and took it as a joke. The king resented his behaviour and said, "Do not take it as a joke. This is our final decision."

On an auspicious day, the princess's marriage with that handicapped person was solemnised. That was the last inauspicious day of the king.

It was a honeymoon night. At mid-night, the king had a small nap. Saturn visited the king in his dream and said, "You ranked me the lowest among the gods. You have undergone enough sufferings for your misjudgement."

The king begged his pardon and said "Please do not inflict such sufferings in future on anyone as you have inflicted upon me." The Saturn accepted the king's request and disappeared.

The king opened his eyes and, to his great surprise, found his hands and feet in proper shape. The princess's joy knew no bounds when she saw her husband in perfect shape. Next day, the king also felt as much happy. And when the king came to know that his son-in-law was no one else but king Vikramaditya himself, he was overwhelmed with joy and praised his stars.

The businessman got this news and felt guilty over his behaviour towards Vikramaditya. He invited him for dinner.

King Vikramaditya said, "I shall dine in the same room where the peg swallowed your precious necklace." The businessman agreed and arranged the dinner in that room.

When the invitees were dining, they saw to their great surprise that the precious necklace was slowly emerging from the same peg. The businessman was so much overwhelmed at this sight that he, too, decided to marry off his daughter to Vikramaditya.

King Vikramaditya returned to his kingdom. He and his two queens were received with full warmth by the subjects.

The king asked his courtiers to make a proclamation by the beat of drum that Saturn is not less powerful than any other god and that they should keep fast on Saturday as a mark of honour of Saturn. Also, they should feed the ants, both in the morning and evening.

Shanivar Ki Kahani- III

(Peepal Worship)

Once there were two sisters - Lakshmi and Daridra. Lakshmi was the goddess of wealth while Daridra was the goddess of poverty. Though they were real sisters, their behaviour towards others and temperament were totally different. Lakshmi got up early in the morning. She took her bath regularly. She remembered God regularly. She took keen interest in her day-to-day work with a smiling face. She befriended everybody and worked till late at night.

Daridra was very lazy. She got up very late. She did not take her bath. Washing clothes was a rare occasion for her. She was very discourteous. She was as much a flirt and unthoughtful. Cruelty and awe were natural to her. She generally told lies and befooled others. She was always hated by men in the street.

Goddess Lakshmi was very much liked by Lord Krishna and he married her happily. Daridra remained alone. She became sad.

One day Lakshmi said to Lord Krishna, "My dear husband, Daridra is my real sister. She is alone. Now she is quite grown up. Please arrange for her marriage. The life of an unmarried woman is difficult in our society."

Lord Krishna said, "My love, your worry is justified. But who will accept her in marriage? Her way of living is hated by one and all. She wears shabby clothes and loiters away her time. Even an ordinary man will not take her hand."

Lakshmi said, "Arrange her marriage with a Rishi. He would not expect much from her because most of his time he would be busy performing religious rites."

Lord Krishna agreed. He searched for a suitable match for Daridra. A Rishi agreed to marry her. Most of the Rishi's disciples were away. He needed someone's help in performing the 'Yajna'.

Goddess Lakshmi was happy that a Rishi had accepted her sister's hand. After performing her marriage, they returned to their kingdom.

Daridra could not accept Rishi's way of life. She would get up late. She would not take her bath. She would not care for the cleanliness of the Ashram. The Rishi was fed up with her indolence. He gave her up.

Daridra was badly disappointed. She went to Lakshmi again. She looked very shabby and disorderly. Lakshmi felt pity for her. She said to Krishna, "Please arrange a suitable abode for her. A woman's life without a suitable abode is difficult. I knew that habits die hard but she has a right to live in this world."

Lord Krishna accepted Lakshmi's request. All the three came down to earth together. Krishna spotted out a Peepal tree in a lonely corner. They went to that tree. Lord Krishna said to Daridra, "You can reside under this tree. This is a lonely place suited to your temperament. You need not clean this place daily. None would visit this place either. You may live as you please."

Daridra said, "I will be fed up with lonely life. Lonely place is an abode of ghosts. Please do visit me frequently with my sister, Lakshmi."

Lord Krishna agreed. He gave a word to her that he would visit and stay at the peepal tree on every Saturday alongwith Lakshmi.

From that day onwards, people visit Peepal tree on every Saturday. They water it and offer their prayers, knowing well that Lord Krishna and Lakshmi reside in the tree on Saturdays.